Table *of* Contents

Mount Moran reflected in Jackson Lake

Introduction

From every direction the Tetons stand out in the landscape. The answer isn't in their particular shape or their role in the history of the West, but in their geology—the story of their rise from deep in the Earth, their erosion, and the formation of the landscape that surrounds them.

What makes them so different? There are higher and more massive peaks in the West. There are ranges of mountains much older and more extensive. Why have these peaks attracted the attention of everyone from prehistoric American Indians to modern day artists? The answer isn't in their particular shape or their role in the history of the West, but in their geology—the story of their rise from deep in the Earth, their erosion, and the formation of the landscape that surrounds them.

First established to preserve the mountains, Grand Teton National Park was later expanded to save the views and open spaces across Jackson Hole's wide sage-brush flats. Early conservationists saw that the contrast between mountain and plain was important, as was the balance of the winding Snake River and the unbroken skyline. Over the years, it became evident that everything contributing to the Grand Teton landscape, from the lakes to the forests to the wildlife, could be traced back to one thing: geology. No matter what attracts you to the park, from fishing to photography, it is based on the processes that built this land.

First-time visitors to these mountains are awed by the peaks, but the series of geologic events that shaped them, and continue to shape them, are just as impressive. These mountains are young compared to the rest of the Rockies, which are more than fifty million years old compared to about thirteen million years for the beginning of the Tetons' rise seven thousand feet up for the mountain side of the fault and about twenty thousand feet down on the valley side. They are still rising and falling, so their story goes on.

The story of the Tetons is a story written in slow motion—a billion years here, a million years there. Take just a few minutes to learn the basic events, and you will find that the rest of the park becomes even more fascinating.

Geology
of Grand Teton National Park

Written by
Charles Craighead

Photography by
Henry H. Holdsworth

**Official Guidebook
of Grand Teton National Park**

Published by
Grand Teton Natural History Association

View east from Signal Mountain, the Snake River in foreground, and beyond to the Absarokas

The Greater Landscape

Gros Ventre Range

The Teton Range covers an area roughly forty miles north and south by fifteen miles east and west, sitting on the western border of Wyoming. Just to the north is Yellowstone National Park. Other, less dramatic mountain ranges surround the Tetons—the Snake River Range to the south, the Gros Ventre Range to the east, the Absarokas to the northeast. Altogether these vast highlands make up a distinct ecosystem of millions of acres surrounded on all sides by a lower, relatively flat region. This island of wild, high country became the last refuge of American bison, a place for grizzly bears and wolves, and home to Native American tribes for thousands of years.

Grand Teton National Park is just a small piece of this geo-ecosystem, more or less centered on the abrupt eastern face of the Teton Range. If you were to stand on the summit of the Grand Teton on a perfectly clear day, you would be able to see the full extent of the greater Teton-Yellowstone region. You would see where it drops away at the north end of Yellowstone, how it slopes downward into Idaho farmland to the west, how it blends into the Wind River Range to the east, and where it breaks up into rolling hills far to the south.

This park is a small part of the land, but at the heart of it all is the Teton fault. An active, but temporarily dormant crack in the Earth's crust, the Teton fault has cut through the land and offset its east and west sides by about five to six vertical miles. This fault made the mountains and the valley, made a path for the glaciers, and helped shape the land for miles around.

5

How the Tetons and Jackson Hole Came to Be

To make a very long story short we need to condense time, skip a number of periods when nothing much happened, and simplify some very complex geological processes. Most of all, we need to condense time. To tell the whole story would take more than one lifetime.

Geologists have learned over the years that the Earth is not a solid ball of rock, but is made of layers around a solid, hot core in the center. (Think of a golf ball or a multi-layered candy jawbreaker.) The inner core of Earth is estimated to be about 12,000 degrees Fahrenheit. The rock gradually gets cooler and more solid toward the outside, where there is a thin layer of hard rock called the lithosphere. In between is the mantle, which is over 700 degrees Fahrenheit where it meets the lithosphere. The whole mantle isn't solid or liquid, but it moves and flows very, very slowly, like warm plastic. The mantle makes up the bulk of the planet, and the lithosphere "floats" on it.

With all the forces at work on the lithosphere, such as the planet spinning, the mantle flowing, and different temperatures here and there, the upper portion of the Earth has broken up into big pieces that geologists call plates. Plates are

A place of contrast—and still changing today

actually made of the crust and the upper mantle, called the lithosphere, and their movements are driven by the heat of the circulating, semi-molten mantle. If we could film the surface of the Earth from space for a few million years and then speed it up, we would see the plates bumping and grinding against each other as they slowly move around. Also, imagine them as big pieces of a puzzle that have gotten mixed up—once they break apart and start moving around, they won't fit together perfectly any more. Plates are extremely massive and powerful, and they slowly crunch each other, ride up over or slide past one another, or get pushed down into the mantle. These plates have been moving around for so long that the continents and seas as we know them are just the latest configuration of the Earth's surface.

To get back to the Tetons, we look at what has happened to the North American Plate. It has been pressured by the Pacific Plate to the west for a long time—they meet along the coast of California—and the Pacific Plate is sliding past us at a rate of a couple inches a year. The infamous San Andreas Fault lies along this border.

There was another earlier plate to the west, the Farallon Plate, that collided with North America before the Pacific Plate. The pressure of the Farallon Plate against the North American Plate gradually caused crumpling and buckling, forming the Rocky Mountains in the time period starting about 120 million years ago and ending about 55 million years ago. The Farallon Plate got pushed under ours (a process called subduction), and it stuck, allowing mountains to be formed far inland. When the sub-plate fell away, it allowed magma to well up, resulting in widespread volcanic activity that created the nearby Absaroka Mountains from 55 to 45 million years ago. After that period of volcanism, there was a lot of residual heat in the crust, and the North American Plate started to stretch and spread back out. As it did, it cracked. This created a vast area named the Basin and Range Province extending from here to the Sierra Nevadas starting a little over 20 million years ago. It is characterized by alternating mountain ranges and valleys.

Heat welling up from beneath North America helped fuel the rise of new mountains. Since the land was being stretched from east to west, the cracks formed north to south. These cracks, called faults, angle deep into the crust. The Teton fault formed this way about thirteen million years ago.

As the land is slowly pulled apart, one side slides down along the fault (the fault isn't perpendicular, but angles steeply downward at about 50 degrees), and the other side rises up. The side that drops down into the mantle displaces some of that material, and it pushes the other side up. Since most of the action is right at the fault, the land that is dropping tends to tilt downward into the fault (the Jackson Hole valley), and the land that is rising tends to tilt up at the fault (the Tetons).

Unfortunately, every time the two blocks of crust move along the fault it creates an earthquake. The Tetons are the result of millions of years' worth of tremendous earthquakes, and it isn't over with yet. The mountains still rise, and the valley still drops.

To visualize the process, compare it to a set of trapdoors: one door swings down to form the valley while the other swings up to form the mountains. The total displacement of the land along the Teton fault is over 27,000 feet.

Not all mountains form this way, but any time you see a range with one steep face and the other side gently sloping, it is likely they were created as the Tetons were. Mountains can also form where two plates push against each other and both buckle upward or where the land rose millions of years ago and everything around it has eroded away. Local ranges, the Gros Ventre and Wind River Mountains to the east and the Snake River Range to the south, formed when the land folded up and eroded.

Teton Range   Teton Fault   Jackson Lake   TETON FAULT

The basic timeline for the formation of the Tetons:

▲ The Earth is formed 4.6 billion years ago.

▲ During the Precambrian Era, about 2.7 to 2.8 million years ago, the collision between ancient continents formed metamorphic gneiss at 20 miles below the Earth's surface.

▲ Shortly after that, about 2.5 million years ago, molten magma squeezed up into cracks in the gneiss to create igneous granite. These ancient core rocks, gneiss and granite, were brought up from deep in the Earth between then and now to form the highest peaks of the Tetons.

▲ Late in the Precambrian Era, about 775 million years ago, magma squeezed into cracks in the ancient core rocks and cooled to form diabase. This is the dark rock that we call the Black Dikes.

▲ The Paleozoic and Mesozoic Eras, when the Teton region was covered with sedimentary rocks—limestone, shale, and sandstone—laid down by shifting seas, 510 to 90 million years ago. The sandstone cap on top of Mount Moran is the first sediment from those seas.

▲ Rise of the Rocky Mountains, including an ancient Teton Range, from compression of North America: 120 to 55 million years ago.

▲ Erosion of the Ancient Teton Range: 70 to 30 million years ago.

▲ Eruptions of Absaroka volcanoes: 55 to 45 million years ago.

▲ Heat underneath North America caused the area to rise and stretch: forming faults and mountains: 20 million years ago.

▲ Formation of the Teton Fault, due to North America stretching: about 10-13 million years ago.

▲ Tetons rise and the valley sinks after the Teton Fault forms. The mountains rise about one foot for every four feet that the valley drops.

▲ Large lake submerges Jackson Hole, depositing 5,000 feet of sediment: 10 million to 5 million years ago.

▲ Yellowstone plume due west of Tetons causes more stretching, fault movement, and Teton uplift.

▲ Ice Age begins: 2 million years ago.

▲ Bull Lake glaciers: 170,000 to 120,000 years ago.

▲ Pinedale glaciers: 50,000 to 14,000 years ago.

▲ Last major earthquake: 4,800 years ago.

▲ Little Ice Age causes modern glaciers in mountains: 1350–1850 A.D.

The Yellowstone Hotspot

One nearby geological feature affecting Grand Teton National Park lies beneath Yellowstone National Park—the Yellowstone Hotspot. A hotspot is a plume of molten rock that rises up from deep in the earth until it reaches the surface. The Hawaiian Islands are formed by volcanic action where the plume of that hotspot erupts through the Pacific Plate. The Yellowstone Hotspot is not connected to the lower mantle and core. Instead, it is a reservoir of molten rock starting about 400 miles down, near the base of the upper mantle. It periodically sends up blobs of molten rock toward the surface, and they melt their way through the upper mantle. These bubbles form magma chambers when

A chamber of molten rock miles below Yellowstone fuels the park's geysers.

they stop rising into the crust. Yellowstone's thermal wonders today are heated by a magma chamber under the park. Occasionally the magma chamber erupts explosive blasts, as happened in Yellowstone roughly 640,000 years ago. Today's magma chamber appears to be stable for now.

Just to complicate things, the North American Plate happens to be moving across the surface of the planet in a southwestward direction. Since the Yellowstone Hotspot is stationary in relation to the center of the Earth, the hotspot appears to us to be burning holes through the crust in a northeastward direction over time. This, in fact, shows up as a trail of old volcanoes leading away from the park into Idaho. In a few million years the hotspot will be in eastern Montana, and Yellowstone may be dormant.

How does all this affect the Teton story? The intense heat of the hotspot causes the Earth's surface to swell up, and once in a while it will blow up and destroy the mountains above it. (Eruptions have buried the northern end of the Tetons under lava and ash). Also, the hotspot's heat and pressure create a zone of active faults around it, including the major Teton fault.

The hotspot was southwest of the Tetons about ten million years ago, due west of the Tetons five million years ago, and reached its present location about two million years ago. This local heat combined with the regional heat from the Basin and Range area appears to have sped up the mountain-building process and provided the energy for the Teton fault to slip and build the jagged, present-day Tetons. This is one of the most seismically active areas of the West, and the Teton fault has a long history of creating big jolts.

Ice Age: Glaciers and Water

Falling Ice Glacier

With the rock of the present-day Tetons in place, it gets a little easier to comprehend the processes that went on here and the timescale. Remember, the Teton story began about thirteen million years ago when the Teton fault formed as this entire area stretched, rose up, and cracked. As the block of crust on the east side sank to form Jackson Hole, it displaced mantle and helped push up the block on the west side to create the Tetons.

Meanwhile, the planet continued on with its processes of change. The climate heated up and cooled off a number of times, and when it cooled two million years ago, there was an Ice Age in northern parts of the world. When this happened, large sheets of glacial ice gradually built up in the north and began to flow southward, only to melt years later when the planet warmed up again. This happened maybe a dozen times to the Teton area in the last two million years. All the while, the Tetons were rising. Each succeeding glacial period tended to bulldoze the landscape and erase all the evidence of the previous period, but we have good evidence of the last two times it happened here. These left the glacial features we see today.

Glaciers form when snow piles up in the mountains or high country and does not melt away in summer. As the snow gradually gets deeper and deeper, it packs down and turns to ice. Eventually, when the ice gets about sixty feet thick, it starts to "flow" slowly downhill on its own. New snow and ice continue to add to the glacier at its head in the mountains, feeding the glacier, making it grow longer and broader, and powering it as it flows out of the high country. During the Ice Age, snow continued to fall on the entire surface of the glacier, so that it also grew deeper and more massive as it flowed.

This is exactly what happened during the Bull Lake period, between about 170,000 and 120,000 years ago. About 3,500 feet of ice built up on the high Yellowstone plateau, which included the Absaroka and Beartooth ranges north of present-day Yellowstone National Park, and began to flow south. It joined ice from the Gros Ventre range to the east, and went as far as the Hoback River south of the present-day town of Jackson. It filled the entire Jackson Hole valley with ice. Signal Mountain, at the south end of Jackson Lake, was buried under nearly 2,000 feet of ice.

Alpine glaciers flowed out of the Tetons and merged with the main ice sheet

Teton Glacier (left)

Diagram of Jackson Hole's glacial times: Hedrick Pond phase of the Pinedale Glaciation.

Labels: Teton Range, Jenny Lake, Signal Mountain, Present-day Jackson Lake, Glacier from the Yellowstone/Absaroka ice mass

during this time.
These smaller glaciers not only carved the canyons into their classic **U**-shapes, but they carried large amounts rock out of the Tetons and dumped it onto the ice sheet in the valley. Thus, massive amounts of rocks and boulders were carted out of the mountains on the top and the base of the ice and left in the valley when the ice eventually melted.

This Bull Lake ice scraped the face of the Teton Range, dug huge basins in the valley, and left moraines and other glacial material throughout the valley.

The most recent period of the Ice Age brought the Pinedale glaciation to the valley. It lasted from roughly 50,000 years ago until about 14,000 years ago and occurred in a few different phases. This ice also flowed out of the high country to the north and east, but it was not nearly as deep, and it only got as far south as Signal Mountain. It joined ice coming down from Yellowstone and carved the 400 foot deep basin containing Jackson Lake. The Pinedale glaciers wiped out much of the evidence of the previous Bull Lake ice to the north. Glaciers also flowed out of the mountain canyons of the Tetons during the Pinedale period, further carving them into their **U**-shapes and bulldozing lake depressions at the canyon mouths.

The latter phase of this Pinedale period, ending 14,000 years ago, put the finishing touches on the landscape as we know it today. We see some of its work as the series of moraines on the valley floor south of Jackson Lake, known as the Burned Ridge Moraine, and the potholes south of Signal Mountain. The moraines are easy to see because they are covered with conifers. The earlier Bull Lake evidence farther south in the valley, such as the glacial moraine called Timbered Island, did not get wiped out by this Pinedale ice. It can still be found, although it is covered by tens of thousands of years worth of windblown soil.

Wherever a glacier reaches its farthest point, it forms a terminal moraine—a pile of rock, clay, and silt that it carried along. As the glacier melts back, it creates a lake in the depression left behind the moraine. Jenny Lake is a good

Water is a slow, steady force of erosion.

example of this. Some glaciers also pile up dirt and rocks along the sides, making lateral moraines as well. Phelps Lake, at the mouth of Death Canyon, sits behind a large lateral moraine. The trail from the Death Canyon Trailhead goes up and over this moraine, providing a great view of the lake and the canyon.

A fresh glacial moraine

When you think about the action of glaciers, you also have to think about what happens when all that ice melts. When we say that the glaciers retreated, it doesn't mean that they reversed direction and flowed back into the mountains—it means that even though they still flowed down they melted, starting at the forward point and working back like a burning candle. Glaciers also melt on the surface and get thinner. Imagine how much water is in a block of ice that could fill this valley thousands of feet deep. As the ice melted, the water washed away almost all the soil, leaving only bare rock in the mountains and cobbles, gravel, and sand in the valley. Periodic floods happened when the ice and rock damming up the meltwater gave way. By driving to the summit of Signal Mountain and looking at the valley floor below, you can see how all that flooding carved the land. There are huge outwash plains, river channels, terraces, and benches from Signal Mountain south.

An erratic—a boulder dropped by a glacier

The glaciers were almost unstoppable, slow-motion bulldozers. They pushed and scraped, and they also acted like conveyor belts carrying rocks and debris on top. Boulders that tumbled onto them from hillsides or mountaintops often ended up miles away when the ice finally melted thousands of years later. These big rocks are called erratics, and they appear all over the park, especially along the base of the Tetons. There are a number of good erratics near Jenny Lake and scattered along the Valley Trail.

Another sign left by the glaciers is the deep grooves, or striations, found in the bedrock in places where it is exposed. This marking is from rocks carried along at the bottom of the glaciers beneath tons and tons of ice, scraping deeply into whatever they went across. Striations can be found most easily at the lower ends of the canyons where bare rock is exposed, such as around Inspiration Point in Cascade Canyon.

From the summit of Signal Mountain, you can see another interesting glacial feature—the Potholes Channelway. Here, meltwater from the Jackson Lake glacier carried outwash debris that covered up big blocks of ice left from an earlier glacial advance. When the blocks melted, they left depressions, or potholes, known as kettles.

Glaciers formed in this high country and flowed into the valley.

Continued Shaping of the Land

The story of Grand Teton National Park's geology has not ended. The Teton fault is still active, meaning that the mountains are still rising and the valley is still sinking. You can see evidence of this above String Lake where the fault has slipped about seventy-five feet since the glaciers melted.

The Earth went through a minor cold spell between about 1350 and 1850 A.D., called the Little Ice Age, when small glaciers formed in the Tetons. (This was roughly the span between the time Columbus landed and when the United States formed.) These glaciers are still present, but are retreating. The power of even a small glacier is evident in the scouring they have done and the moraines they have created. Twelve glaciers are found in the Tetons, and many can be seen from the highway. Most prominent are the Teton Glacier, just to the right of the Grand Teton, and the Falling Ice and Skillet glaciers on the face of Mount Moran.

Ice continues to work on the Tetons on a much smaller scale as well. Every winter, ice forms from snow in the mountains, and moves rocks inch by inch as it freezes and thaws. Rocks are cracked and eventually broken when water seeps into crevices in the rock then freezes and expands, a process called frost wedging.

The water that results each spring when snow melts is another powerful force in the mountains. It moves material downhill bit by bit, erodes the soil holding rocks in place, and very slowly erodes bare rock as it carries abrasive silt and gravel.

Ice, water, and wind: these forces work together on a timescale we cannot often witness. But if you were to stand on the Teton Glacier beneath the North Face of the Grand Teton on a spring day or after a summer rainstorm, you would hear the steady clatter of falling rocks.

The final force affecting the Tetons is the same one that formed them: earthquakes. This is a seismically active area, and periodic quakes shake the park. There have been no quakes in the last 4,800 years as powerful as the massive earthquakes that occurred during the early formation of the mountains. Most geologists predict that more large earthquakes will happen along the Teton Fault and are, in fact, overdue, but no one can predict when.

Cirque

Glacier

Moraine

Outwash plain

Cutaway view of a classic glacier

Meltwater continues to shape the Tetons.

Glacial cobble

Rock Types in the Park

Most of the rock in the Tetons can be divided into two groups: the ancient building blocks that were formed billions of years ago and the more recent rocks that were made by inland seas covering those ancient rocks starting about 510 million years ago.

Ancient Rocks: Most of the rock you see when you look up at the Tetons is gneiss, which is a metamorphic rock made from other, even older rocks. It formed about twenty miles deep in the Earth's crust under extreme pressure and heat. There are several kinds of gneiss here, and most of them have distinct layers that give a banded appearance to the rock. At one point in its formation, gneiss was pliable, like taffy or modeling clay, and it got twisted and folded before it hardened. You can see these folded layers in much of the exposed gneiss. The layers are composed of such things as quartz, feldspar, and biotite, with occasional horneblende and magnetite. These rocks formed from other types of rocks such as sedimentary and volcanic rocks during the collision of ancient tectonic plates. A hike into Paintbrush Canyon or to Inspiration Point will reveal some gneiss.

Besides these layered kinds of gneiss, there are other types of metamorphic rocks that occur in smaller outcroppings or in specific sites. Soapstone, serpentinite, talc, and other metamorphic rocks show up here and there. The various kinds of metamorphic rocks originated from different kinds of previous rock, giving them a variety of properties. Whatever the original rocks were, all were metamorphosed billions of years ago.

The other type of ancient rock is igneous rock, which was once magma, or molten rock. Since it was a heated to a consistent mix, it has no layers, but as it cooled and hardened it formed into a grainy, crystalline texture. Granite is an igneous rock that makes up the central core of the Tetons—the Grand Teton and the other highest peaks. This particular granite is called Mount Owen Quartz Monzonite, and it is mostly light gray or white and fine-grained. It looks speckled as opposed to the layered look of the gneiss. The high, jagged central peaks of the Tetons look like they do because they are made of this hard, erosion-resistant granite.

The Grand Teton, with a black dike in the notch at left.

The Black Dikes: On several of the peaks, especially Mount Moran and the Middle Teton, you can see another type of igneous rock called diabase. A contrasting line of dark rock cuts up through the face of both of these peaks. Like other igneous rocks, the diabase was molten at one point when it was deep in the Earth. As the bedrock shifted and moved beneath the surface, about 775 million years ago, the diabase was squeezed into vertical cracks that formed in the granite and gneiss. It cooled and solidified and was uplifted along with all the other rocks when the Tetons rose.

There are also many granite and pegmatite dikes that were squeezed into the bedrock gneiss in the same fashion. They formed at the same time that the granite did and are generally much smaller and look more like the surrounding rock than the large black dikes do.

More Recent Rocks: Another way rocks can form is when wind or water transport or precipitate sand, silt, or other materials. These sediments are buried deeper and deeper as the layers build up. Eventually, after millions of years, the immense pressure squeezes them into flat layers of rock. These are named sedimentary rocks for the obvious reason that they formed from sediments. Sandstone and limestone are two of the sedimentary rocks found here. These are the kinds of rock that once covered this entire area, before the mountains rose and the softer sedimentary rocks eroded away.

Sandstone is created when sand is compressed until it turns to stone. There are other rocks similiar to sandstone, including siltstone made from silt and shale from clay.

Limestone forms when minerals precipitate out of the seawater and settle on the bottom, or when shells, corals, and other living organisms die and build up on the sea floor. Eventually they get buried deeper and deeper and get compressed into stone. Limestone is often full of fossils, the remains of shells, fish, and other living organisms that turned to rock along with the minerals.

Limestone formations, upper Granite Canyon

Sedimentary rocks made up the flat landscape here before the Tetons rose. When that happened, they began to erode away, leaving only the hard granite and gneiss to slowly weather into the peaks we see today. These sedimentary rocks are readily visible along the southern part of the Tetons, but in the central part they are eroded away. If you hike up into Alaska Basin on the west side of the peaks you can see it all—limestone, sandstone, and the rugged Teton peaks. You can also travel east out of the valley into the Gros Ventre River drainage and see the same layered rocks that once covered the Tetons. And, if you look carefully at Mount Moran, you can see a little light brown patch of sandstone on its top—one remaining bit of the overlying land that was raised by the Teton fault.

A dike of black diabase on Middle Teton

Precious Minerals, Gems, and Interesting Rocks

Magnetite spots in "bright-eyed" gneiss

Flakes of mica

Obsidian

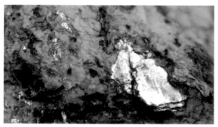

Volcanic rock (16" dia.) was mixed in with glacial cobble, rounded by ice and water.

No one ever got rich mining or prospecting in this valley, even before the park was established and those activities were stopped. Gold miners in the late 1800s and early 1900s tried all kinds of ways to concentrate the fine gold dust they found all through the valley, but the effort wasn't worth it. At one point, in the early 1870s, miners dug a ditch all the way across Antelope Flats for their placer mine along the Snake River. Tiny flakes and gold dust are all that anyone ever found.

Garnet Canyon is named for the large garnets that have been found there, but they are not valuable as gems. They have fractures and impurities but are interesting to see. Large crystalline flakes of mica can also be found.

Early American Indians collected obsidian, black volcanic glass used for knives and points, in the southern Teton Range near Teton Pass; at the north end of the range; and in Yellowstone, but not in the main part of the Teton Range. They also found areas of soapstone for their bowls and pipes in the Teton Range.

Plagioclase feldspar band in gneiss.

Major Peaks of the Teton Range

Static Peak (L) and Buck Mountain (R)

Static Peak

11,303 ft.
Named for its frequent lightning strikes.

Buck Mountain

Buck Mountain

11,938 ft.
Topographer George A. Buck built a cairn on top in 1898, named "Buck Station." A large fault lies west of the peak, shoving ancient gneiss over younger sedimentary rocks.

Mount Wister and Veiled Peak

Veiled Peak

11,330 ft.
Hidden behind the larger peaks.

Mount Wister

11,490 ft.
Named after Owen Wister, author of *The Virginian* and an early visitor to Jackson Hole.

Albright Peak   Static   Buck Mt.   Wister   South Teton   Middle Teton   Grand Teton

South Teton

South Teton

12,514 ft.
Named for its location among the other high peaks. Composed mostly of ancient metamorphic gneiss.

Middle Teton

Middle Teton

12,804 ft.
Named for its location among the other high peaks. Has a prominent black dike that forms a slot in the granite as the softer diabase erodes.

Nez Perce

Nez Perce

11,901 ft.
Named for Nez Perce Indians who hunted in this region.

Cathedral Group with the Grand Teton in middle

Grand Teton

13,770 ft.
Renamed Mt. Hayden after Ferdinand V. Hayden but the name didn't stick. Mostly granite.

Grand Teton
Mount Owen
Teew

Sketch from 1872 Hayden Survey

Mount Owen

Mount Owen

12,928 ft.
Named for William Owen. The igneous "granite" is named Mount Owen Quartz Monzonite for this mountain.

Teewinot Mountain

Teewinot Mountain

12,325 ft.
Name comes from the Shoshone Indian word "Tee-Win-At" meaning "pinnacles." Beautiful outcrops of granite cutting across gneiss.

Mount St. John

Mount St. John

11,430 ft.
Named for Orestes H. St. John, geologist with the 1872 Hayden Expedition.

Mount St. John
Rockchuck Peak
Mount Moran
Mount Woodring
Cottonwood Creek

Rockchuck Peak

Rockchuck Peak

11,144 ft.
Named for marmots, commonly
called woodchucks.

Mount Woodring

Mount Woodring

11,590 ft.
Named for the first superintendent
of Grand Teton National Park,
Samuel T. Woodring.

Mount Moran

Mount Moran

12,605 ft.
Named for landscape artist Thomas
Moran. A smorgasbord of geology:
glaciers, Flathead sandstone on top, a
massive black dike, and gneiss with
some granite.

The meandering Snake River cuts into the glacial cobble. (overleaf)

Major Geologic Features of the Park

Modern Glaciers

Teton Glacier and Mt. Owen

The Little Ice Age, in the years between about 1350 and 1850 A.D. formed small glaciers high in the Tetons. They have been receding for many years but might still be active. A few of these are visible from turnouts along the Teton Park Road. The Teton Glacier is best seen from the Teton Glacier Turnout on the Teton Park Road or from the Glacier View Turnout on Highway 89/191.

Two glaciers are prominent on Mount Moran—Falling Ice Glacier and Skillet Glacier. Falling Ice is visible from the Cathedral Group turnout or the Mount Moran turnout, while Skillet Glacier is easier to see from across Jackson Lake, at Jackson Lake Dam, or Colter Bay.

Although small in comparison to the prehistoric ice that once filled the valley, these modern glaciers behave the same way and produce the same kinds of moraines, rock scarring, and scouring that the big ones did. Most of the lakes in the alpine community are found in cirques that glaciers carved at the head of a canyon or the flank of a mountain.

Canyons

Cascade Canyon

One feature making the Tetons accessible to hikers and climbers is the array of canyons cutting through the high peaks. These formed from a combination of erosion by water and glacial activity plus a lot of time. The canyons were initially carved by streams flowing out of the mountains, but much of their shape today is from the glacial ice that slowly widened and deepened the canyons. Evidence of this action is seen in the U-shape of the canyons, typical of glacier activity, and polished, scarred, striated rock on the canyon walls and base.

The canyons are not only good places to access the Teton back country; they are great places to get a cross-section view of the mountain range. One unusual characteristic of these canyons is that they cut back so deeply into

Falling Ice Glacier

Upper Cascade Canyon Trail

the Tetons that they reveal the structure of the mountains. This occurred because the mountains rose so quickly, and ice and water sliced canyons into the bedrock like a knife into butter.

Death Canyon and Paintbrush Canyons are both good places to see the different kinds of gneiss that make up the Teton Range. These rocks are visible in the lower canyons where glacial activity cut deeply into the bedrock. Paintbrush Divide is a good place to see granite (quartz monzonite).

Moraines

Phelps Lake moraine near Death Canyon

Another sign left by the glaciers is the series of terminal moraines, one for just about every canyon, that form lakes where the canyon glaciers met the valley floor. Jenny, Taggart and Bradley lakes are good examples of these "piedmont" lakes that form behind a terminal moraine. Phelps Lake also has a large lateral moraine that formed along the side of the glacier as it came out of Death Canyon. You will notice a southward curve to that moraine, formed when the Death Canyon glacier merged with the massive Bull Lake glacier filling the entire valley. The resulting Pinedale/Bull Lake moraine is an interesting and easy destination for a hike.

Since the moraines are composed of rock, clay, and silt carried by the glacial ice, they retain moisture and tend to create better soil for plants. This is evident in the forests surrounding each lake.

Other moraines, such as the Burned Ridge moraine in the flats south of Jackson Lake, are also made conspicuous by their covering growth of trees. These moraines are easily visible from the summit of Signal Mountain.

Timbered Island, on the east side of the Teton Park Road and south of the Jenny Lake area, is a long medial moraine formed during the Bull Lake period as alpine glaciers from the mountains merged with the valley ice sheet. The difference between its soil and that of the surrounding flat glacial outwash is obvious.

If you want to see a terminal moraine up close, hike the Taggart Lake Trail. This area was burned by a wildfire and is slowly recovering, but meanwhile the rocks, boulders, and shape of the moraine are all clearly visible. These moraines are hummocky due to the pulses of ice when the glacier reached its maximum extent.

Lakes

String Lake

Most of the lakes in Grand Teton National Park are glacial in origin. The high altitude lakes, such as Amphitheater Lake, Surprise Lake, and Lake Solitude, are cirque lakes formed when small glaciers scoured out deep little basins. The string of lakes along the base of the mountains, including Jenny, Leigh, and Taggart lakes, are piedmont lakes formed by the glaciers that once flowed out of the canyons. When these glaciers reached the valley floor, they dug out deep depressions and piled up terminal moraines.

Emma Matilda and Two Ocean lakes are the oldest glacial lakes in the park, filling depressions scoured by Pinedale glaciers about 20,000 to 25,000 years ago.

Jackson Lake, the largest lake in the park, lies in a very deep hole scoured by ice during the Pinedale glaciation that ended about 14,000 years ago. The glaciers originally dug a hole about 800 feet deep, and it has since filled in with almost 400 feet of sediment.

The Valley Floor

Setting off the dramatic rise of the Tetons, the flat valley floor looks as if it were poured into place, and it practically was. As the mountains rose and the valley dropped along the Teton fault, the valley gradually filled in with material eroded off the mountains, carried in by glaciers, and washed in from surrounding high country. What we see on top is mostly cobbles of ancient metamorphic quartzite rock worn smooth and round from being cycled through the geologic record many times.

It is interesting to walk around on the flats to find places where the cobbles are exposed. Near any of the scenic turnouts along Highway 89/187 or along the Teton Park Road, you can wander through the nearby sagebrush and look at the cobbles. You'll be surprised to see how many different kinds of rock, from granite to quartzite to volcanic, have been worn into smooth, round rocks. Many of these cobbles are a type of metamorphic rock called quartzite formed by heating and compressing sandstone into a very hard rock that resists being worn away as it was tumbled during the glacial melt.

If we could strip away this fill material, the park would be a much different place. We would be able to see the total offset created by the Teton fault, and it would be an awesome sight. Geologists estimate that the valley floor dropped some 20,000 feet at the fault, while the mountains rose about 7,000 feet above the present-day valley floor. So if you were to stand in the high-

The flat valley floor meets the Tetons.

lands the east of the park you would be looking into a deep valley, and the mountains that rose out of the valley would rise steeply upward from the Teton fault.

Rivers and Streams

Snake River

Geology determined the course of the park's rivers and streams as well as its lakes. The Snake River, winding down the center of the valley, originates in southern Yellowstone, flows into Jackson Lake and out of the southeast end of the lake. It follows old glacial patterns in the valley left tens of thousands of years ago. The glaciers that scoured out Jackson Lake left moraines piled up at its south end, and after flowing directly south for a time, the water eroded a lower point at its present outlet. Jackson Lake Dam now controls that outlet. From the dam to Pacific Creek, the Snake flows eastward in a basin scoured during the early Pinedale glaciation, then turns south and follows the path of old glacial outwash. As the glaciers melted, vast amounts of water flowed through the valley, creating channels that are now

39

dried up. They are still easily visible from the air or from the top of Signal Mountain.

At times, ice dams or moraines held back the meltwater until it was released in a flood, cutting a wide swath through outwash material of the valley floor. The present-day Snake River flows between pairs of terraces marking old melts and floods. It cuts a wide riverbottom as it meanders back and forth in the loose gravel and cobble of the valley.

Streams coming into the Snake from the east have their headwaters in the highlands outside the park. The Gros Ventre River, Buffalo Fork, Pacific Creek, Spread Creek, and Ditch Creek all cut across the glacial outwash to empty into the Snake. On the west side, most of the streams originate in the Tetons from springs, melting snow and ice spill into the piedmont lakes at the base of the mountains, and then flow on to the Snake River at some point. Cottonwood Creek is the most prominent. It begins at the outlet of Jenny Lake where a small gap in the moraine lets water out and then angles southeast to meet the Snake just upstream of Moose. The streams along the base of the Tetons don't flow directly into the Tetons but hug the base of the mountains because movement on the Teton fault has created a sag or depression next to the mountains that the streams follow.

Surrounding Mountain Ranges

Although not as spectacular as the Tetons, significant but older mountain ranges surround Grand Teton National Park in all directions. Just south of the park the Teton Range gives way to the Snake River Range, composed of

Snake River Range, south of the Tetons

Aerial view of Blacktail Butte, with Timbered Island in the background.

layered limestone and sandstone. Beyond that lie the Hoback, Salt River, and Wyoming ranges. To the north, the Teton Range disappears into the high Yellowstone Plateau, where previous mountains were destroyed by volcanic eruptions and then buried under more recent volcanic flows.

Southeast of the park is the the Gros Ventre Range, a rugged area marked on the west end by Sheep Mountain (also known as the Sleeping Indian). The rock layers of the Gros Ventres are the same sedimentary rocks found on the south and west sides of the Tetons (the core of the Gros Ventres is also granite like the Tetons). To the north of the Gros Ventres lies the vast wilderness of the Absaroka and Washakie Ranges. This high country was the source of much of the glacial ice that flowed through Jackson Hole during past ice ages and was formed from the ancient volcanic activity of fifty-five million years ago. The Absaroka Range is eroded layers of lava and volcanic debris.

Buttes

One interesting geological feature of the Jackson Hole valley is the series of buttes that rise like islands out of the flat plain. Blacktail Butte sits dead center in the valley with its northern tip near Moose. This butte is a remnant of the valley bedrock that did not sink down with the rest of the land on the east side of the Teton fault. It was formed by a bend in the Teton fault that left this piece of bedrock sitting up high. Carved into its shape by flowing glaciers and glacial outwash, it is now surrounded by glacial outwash.

The Gros Ventre country just to the east of the park (overleaf)

41

Geology and Life

By the time the Bull Lake glacial period ended, about 120,000 years ago, this entire valley and the mountain canyons had been buried under thousands of feet of ice for almost 50,000 years. It is hard to imagine that anything could have survived except for a few hardy alpine plants that may have held on in the high country above the ice. None of the wildlife associated with Grand Teton National Park today—elk, bears, moose, bison—could have lived here.

The second glacial episode, the Pinedale period that ended about 14,000 years ago, reached the south end of Jackson Lake and again flooded the valley floor with melting ice for a long period as it ended. But, archeological evidence shows that early Native Americans visited the valley to fish, gather plants, and hunt as early as 11,000 years ago, when glaciers in the canyons of the Tetons would still have been there. How did the plants come back in that time interval to begin creating new natural communities that would attract both wildlife and humans?

Since soil is the key to plant life, the geologic process of soil formation was the most important factor in bringing the valley back to life. Where and how soil formed over the millennia determined where plants live in the park today. The life-supporting soil of the park was created in several ways.

First, the glaciers stripped away tons and tons of soil and carried it with them. When the ice melted, some soil was left behind. Much of this washed away, but a little of it remained in the moraines, on hillsides covered with glacial till, and as sediments in lakes. This is where windblown plant seeds first took root.

Plant and animal life find a toehold in Jackson Hole.

A lot of the soil that washed away in the melting ice went down the Snake River channels and out into the plains of Idaho. Some of this eventually was blown back as windblown soil, or loess, and settled in layers where the winds dropped it. Today, many coyote and badger dens are found in this loess because it isn't full of glacial cobbles and is easier to dig.

Badger

New soil formed in this region from the mechanical and chemical break-down of rocks, called weathering. This happened through the breakup of rocks from roots, ice and the chemical action of lichens on the rocks.

Even taken altogether, there has not been a lot of soil built up. The deepest areas are on the eastern side of the park where soil from the surrounding highlands eroded into the valley. So the process of establishing new plant life and subsequent animal life followed the patterns of geologic soil formation. These patterns are evident today in forests, meadows, and other plant communities.

For the most part, plants first arrived here as seeds on the wind. Prevailing winds in this area come from the southwest, and since the glacial ice did not reach any farther south than this, the land south of here was still covered with vegetation. Those lower areas outside the high Teton and Yellowstone country were also where the early Native American visitors came from.

As the Ice Age ended, Jackson Hole had only small alpine plants, appearing more like arctic tundra. By the time the Paleoindians arrived, there were grasses, small shrubs such as willows, and wildflowers. Plants could not thrive

Gros Ventre Slide

until the establishment of a few species of nitrogen-fixing plants—these plants are able to live in poor soil and prepare it for later species. Likewise, trees could not become established, even on the moraines, until spores of certain fungi blew in on the wind and established themselves in the soil to help the trees absorb nitrogen.

In the park today, you can see how the basic underlying geology, the formation of soil, and the work of the glaciers determined where plants, wildlife, and humans live.

Sagebrush Flats: The broad, flat expanse of the valley floor is almost all glacial outwash of one period or another. It is composed of sand, gravel, cobble, and very little soil. Water drains quickly through it. Sagebrush, grasses, and other small plants are all that can grow in this sandy soil.

Moraines: Distributed along the base of the mountains, surrounding lakes, and marking the passage of glaciers across the flats, the old moraines contain enough silt, clay, and mineral nutrients for plants to take root and thrive. The fine-grained silt and clay in the moraines also had the capacity to retain moisture, allowing conifers to take root.

Meadows: A few meadows mark the sites of old glacial-period lakes and potholes, where sediments created a rich, moist area. Present-day lakes are often surrounded by areas of meadows in rich soil that was once part of a larger lake. Other meadows mark more recent sites where soil that formed or collected at higher elevations has washed down to flat, low-lying areas.

Forests: On the moraines, in the lower canyons, and on the lower slopes of the mountains, enough soil has built up to support trees and more precipitation falls on the mountains. There are also forests that line the Snake River and other streams. Again, they mark where deeper soil has collected. You can see this need for soil clearly on exposed places like the west side of Blacktail Butte (facing the mountains). Here, the south facing slopes are almost bare, and the north facing slopes are thick with trees. The collection of windblown soil, accumulating here like drifting snow, and the retention of moisture make these slopes ideal for trees. Also, the southern facing slopes get baked by the sun and lose their moisture.

Wildlife: Animals are ultimately dependent on plants, so the distribution of wildlife corresponds to the distribution of plants. The glacial outwash flats are home to sagebrush and grass and attract pronghorn, bison, and coyotes. The forested moraines are home to black bears, elk, deer, and numerous birds. The rockfall areas in the mountains are home to pikas and marmots. The waterways cutting through outwash are inhabited by beavers, otters, Bald Eagles, and trout. Each geologic site, with its soil, wind and water, exposure to the sun, and elevation, has certain plants that support specific animals. By learning the basic geology and its effect on plants, you can more easily find the wildlife of the park.

Humans: Just like the wildlife, early human residents of Jackson Hole looked for certain conditions for their survival—plants, water, and protection from the elements. If you think in terms of what humans need. You will see that settlement occurred at lower elevations where the topsoil was best, where there was good water, and where transportation was feasible. Sites where these geologic conditions combine are few, and those places are where the first permanent people settled. In the park such places as Mormon Row, Cottonwood Creek, and the Moran area mark sites where the geology was right for homesteading. The geology of these sites even dictated what kinds of fences the homesteaders could build. Buck and rail fences, common throughout the valley, don't require fence posts driven into the hard, cobble-filled ground.

Oxbow Bend, near the outlet of Jackson Lake.

Special Sites for Observation

Signal Mountain Summit

This is probably the best all-around site for observing and understanding the geology of the Tetons and Jackson Hole. From this height it is easy to see the contrast between the flat valley floor and the Tetons. Where they meet roughly marks the Teton fault, the focal point of the energy that formed the mountains. Remember that the valley dropped roughly four times the amount that the mountains rose, but all that difference is buried by the sediments filling the valley. Mount Moran, with Skillet Glacier, dominates the skyline. Jackson Lake lies between the Tetons and Signal Mountain, and the terminal glacial moraine that impounded the lake 15,000 years ago is on the south end, covered with trees. The long ridge of pines extending out into the flats is Burned Ridge, an older moraine from the Pinedale period.

In the flats below are dozens of potholes, small ponds and depressions that formed when pieces of ice that broke off the retreating glaciers were buried in the outwash and later melted to leave behind large depressions in the ground.

To the north you can see the Yellowstone Plateau and the Absaroka Range, both sources of glaciers in past ages. Directly below Signal Mountain, the

View from Signal Mountain

Snake River leaves Jackson Lake and heads east, then turns south to follow the valley. Two lakes, Two Ocean and Emma Matilda, lie just over a small ridge to the north. And away to the east you can see the Mt. Leidy high-lands and the Gros Ventre Range—land that was once part of the rock formations covering the Tetons before they rose.

The top of Signal Mountain itself is covered with cobbles left by the Bull Lake glaciers.

Teton Fault Scarp

Earth movement is revealed.

From the Cathedral Group turnout near the North Jenny Lake Junction, you can see evidence of the still active Teton fault. If you look west, toward the Tetons, in the afternoon you'll see a crescent-shaped scarp in a steep, grassy slope at the bottom of Rockchuck Peak. This part of the hill is glacial material, so the fault has moved that much since the glaciers melted about 14,000 years ago. The scarp is about 125 feet high, but the fault actually slipped 75 feet.

Gros Ventre Slide

From the Antelope Flats Road you can get a good look at the Gros Ventre slide, just outside the park to the east. It is a large landslide on the north side of Sheep Mountain, where in 1925, fifty million cubic yards of rock, the largest slide in North America (other than Mt. St. Helens), roared down the mountain and dammed the Gros Ventre River.

The Gros Ventre Slide, days after it occurred

Two years later the dam broke, destroying the town of Kelly, killing six people, and flooding Wilson, 18 miles away.

Ditch Creek Fan

Alluvial fans form where a stream drains high country of its sediment-laden water in the form of mudflows or debris flows and deposits those sediments when it spreads out on the valley floor. The Ditch Creek fan formed after the glaciers receded and left a barren land. Erosion filled the creek with silt, clay, sand, and gravel, and they were

View east toward the source

carried all the way to Blacktail Butte. The Ditch Creek fan holds the deepest topsoil in the park, and was a prized location for early homesteaders.

Blacktail Butte

A remnant of the ancient bedrock that sank along the Teton fault to form Jackson Hole, this butte is a fascinating island in the middle of the flat outwash plain. Sculpted by glaciers and shaped by old stream deposits, the butte is a great model for study. You can drive completely around it, observing how the different faces that contain different kinds of rock have responded to the elements.

The east side of Blacktail Butte

The popular "climbing wall" at the northwest end of Blacktail Butte is composed of sedimentary layers turned on end. Fossils can be seen in these rocks.

Glacier View Turnout or Teton Glacier Turnout

View up Glacier Gulch

The most visible modern glacier is the Teton Glacier, and with a decent pair of binoculars or a spotting scope, you can study the classic features of a mountain glacier. The pile of bare, fresh looking rock and gravel just below it is the terminal moraine. This is what much of the Jackson Hole valley looked like when the big glaciers melted. Except for a brief advance in the 1960s and early 1970s, this glacier has been retreating ever since it has been observed by humans.

Snake River Overlook

From high on an ancient terrace

This scenic turnout gives a nice view across the Snake River toward the mountains, revealing how the river has cut a winding path along the glacial debris of the river bottom. You can also see the different levels of terraces marking ancient flooding of the river by glacial melt. Off toward Mount Moran you can see a slightly raised area of pine forest. This is the Burned Ridge Moraine that the Snake River cut through thousands of years ago.

Oxbow Bend

Slow-moving waters of the oxbow

The Snake River at one time flowed through this channel, but now the main current runs close to the base of Signal Mountain. The oxbow will eventually be completely cut off from the river water and will become a lake. Since the valley floor is tilted toward the mountains, the river is having to cut against the land until it turns south again. Signal Mountain is tilting west along with the valley floor. It is covered with glacial debris and cobbles and has bands of volcanic rock from two of the gigantic Yellowstone eruptions millions of years ago.

Grand Teton Park Sign Turnout

This relatively high spot at the southern border to the park is a good place to orient yourself to the Jackson Hole valley. If you face north from here, away from the town of Jackson, the park extends as far north as you can see. The Tetons, across the valley to your left, get progressively higher to the north until reaching the 13,770 foot height of the Grand Teton. Warm springs bubble up along an old fault from the base of the hill to your left (East Gros Ventre Butte), and its cliffs are volcanic andesite.

Jackson Lake Dam

Jackson Lake used to drain from the south end, from Spalding Bay, but a glacial moraine blocked that exit. The water then cut a new path through softer sediments where the dam is now located. The original dam was built in the early 1900s, but it washed out. The current dam raises the lake 39 feet above its natural level. Jackson Lake was scoured out of the valley by glaciers, first by one from the east that flowed down the Pacific Creek valley, and later by a large glacier from the Yellowstone Plateau that flowed along the base of the mountains. The latter one cut a basin 800 feet deep, but it partially filled in with sediments so the lake is now just over 400 feet deep.

Mount Moran Turnout

Mount Moran is a huge block of the ancient bedrock gneiss and some granite that rose to form the Tetons over the past thirteen million years. While it was still deep in the Earth's crust, molten rock was forced into cracks in the gneiss and then hardened into a dike of black rock called diabase. This is the dark vertical streak you see at the top of the peak. It is about 150 feet wide and extends for six to seven miles west through the Tetons. On top, just to the right of the dike, is a light brown patch

Mount Moran

of sandstone. This is all that's left of the layers of sedimentary rock that once covered this entire area before the Tetons rose and eroded away.

Also visible on Mount Moran are several modern glaciers. Falling Ice Glacier is wedged into a steep gulch toward the top of the mountain, and its moraine tumbles down the face of the peak. To the right is Skillet Glacier. You can see how much sculpting can be done, even by two small glaciers.

©2006 Grand Teton Natural History Association
Grand Teton National Park
P.O. Box 170, Moose WY 83012
www.grandtetonpark.org

Series Design by
Jeff Pollard Design & Associates
and
Ormsby & Thickstun Interpretive Design

Maps by
Mike Reagan

Project Coordinated by
Jan Lynch, Executive Director,
Grand Teton Natural History Association

Printed by
Paragon Press

ISBN 978-0-931895-68-5